I0180468

Cover Photo by Tomáš Nožina on Unsplash
Copyright © by Gramercy Park Press - All rights reserved.
Cover Photo by Tomáš Nožina on Unsplash

BARCELONA

The Food Enthusiast's Long Weekend Guide

Table of Contents

INTRODUCTION

Barcelona, Spain's second biggest city, is one of the most visited cities in Europe with many millions of tourists visiting annually. And I am most definitely one of them. Barcelona, known for the splendid Modernism architecture of **Antoni Gaudi**, is arguably just as much the city of **Picasso** and **Miro**. The city boasts gorgeous beaches, serene parks, lovely gardens, a preserved medieval historic quarter and fine museums, but many visit Barcelona for the gastronomical delights. Barcelona is a city to be explored and there's no better way to explore and discover the culture than through its distinctive cuisine.

LOCAL CUISINE

Barcelona is a foodies' paradise and food is taken very seriously. You'll find an endless variety of great restaurants from 5-star eateries, molecular experimental to traditional Catalan and Basque. The many food markets offer everything from fresh fruits and vegetables, breads, and olive oil. The popular Catalan cuisine, an ancient Mediterranean style, is characterized by local herbs, meats, and seafood. Food is number one and people often plan supper while eating lunch or scheduling their day around what they're going to eat. Spanish food is delicious and quite healthy. The town is literally a buffet offering a variety of cuisine, including **tapas** (there are tapas bars everywhere) and **paella** – a rich dish that's very popular although it comes from Valencia. The best paella is served in the **Barceloneta** area.

In Barcelona, as you will quickly see on your very first night here, time means nothing and locals eat late, drink late and party all night long. Some clubs open as some people are getting up and going to work. Barcelona's bar scene thrived in the 1980s and has continued with a wealth of trendy lounges and cocktail bars. There's certainly a bar to suit every mood and cocktail preference, whether you're strictly a beer and ale drinker or prefer a vintage-style bar that serves the classic Dry Martini.

EAT LIKE A LOCAL

Locals generally begin their day with a café con leche (coffee with milk) and a piece of toast. The real breakfast comes much later (around 11a.m.) and is more substantial, like a sandwich or croissant. Lunch is late, so if you eat lunch at noon you'll be dining with tourists. Around 4 or 5 p.m., locals will have a real meal – appetizer, main course and dessert. Dinner, often lasting several hours, is usually around 9 or 10 p.m. or even later. Of course, if you're on a different schedule, grab some tapas, everyone's favorite. Tapas bars are everywhere in Barcelona.

When visiting the local restaurants always check the reviews and look for the "Menú del día" (Menu of the day), daily specials usually at a better value. Sometimes you can get 3 courses (first, main and dessert) with bread and beverage (wine, beer, or water) for one price. Coffee is rarely included.

English-speaking tourists fill the restaurants in Barcelona so the local eateries are accommodating. Many restaurants will have menus in three languages: English, Castellano and Catalan. Please note: you might want to compare the Spanish side of the menu with the English side. Translations can be confusing but often the waiters, if they speak English, will try to explain.

Barcelona restaurants run the gamut from barrios to Michelin restaurants (Barcelona boasts a handful of two-star Michelin restaurants and almost 2 dozen one-star restaurants.) Some of these places are expensive, but not all of them. Some popular eateries to check out include: **TICKETS** – a beautifully decorated bar and restaurant in the Poble Sec barrio serving passionfruit-flavored marshmallow worms; **BODEGA 1900** – a classic vermouth bar; **CAELUM** – a pastry and confectionary shop in the Gothic

Quarter selling jam jars, cakes and biscuits; **PUDDING** – a colorful coffee shop with a tempting array of cakes and muffins; and **TORRE DE ALTA MAR** – a tourist favorite located 250-feet above sea level offering incredible city views and delicious herring caviar.

EXPLORING THE CITY

Don't miss a stroll on **La Rambla**, the most famous street in Barcelona, which is actually 5 boulevards joined to make one long promenade, that starts at Placa Catalunya and ends at the Columbus statue by the waterfront. Thousands of people wander down Las Ramblas every day and evening. You can enjoy performing artists, shop, or sit at one of the many outdoor cafes. Another street not to miss, **Portal de l'Angel Avenue**, possibly the busiest street in Barcelona because of its many shops and cafes;

however, it's also known as the most expensive street in Spain.

CULTURE AND MUSEUMS

Barcelona is rich in history and culture and the **City History Museum**, set in a medieval building (once a royal residence), offers a unique opportunity to explore the historical heritage of the city. The museum's headquarters can be found on Placa del Rei in the Gothic Quarter but the museum governs a number of historic buildings around the city, many archaeological sites displaying the ruins of the ancient city. Others include old industrial buildings and sites – many related to architect Antoni Gaudi and the Spanish Civil War.

The National Museum of Art of Catalonia, located in the Palau Nacional of Montjulic, houses a collection of Romanesque art – with the best collection of Romanesque mural painting in the world – and some of the greats of Catalan Modernism such as Gaudi and Casas. The building itself is a marvel to view, constructed for the International Exposition of 1929, the façade is topped with a large dome and two lesser domes on either side and four towers inspired by the Cathedral of Santiago de Compostella. Located on the hill of Montjulic, the museum offers incredible views of Barcelona. (On my last trip I got lost trying to find the restaurant on the upper level and ended up on top of the whole massive structure—on the roof—what a view! I take first time visitors to this restaurant so they can enjoy the view.) The museum holds over 290,000 works of art including Catalan Modernism,

Gothic art, and great European Renaissance and Baroque painters like Tiziano and Velazquez.

The Barcelona Museum of Contemporary Art, known as MACBA, located in the Plaça del Àngels, in El Raval, Ciutat Vella, features a permanent collection of approximately 5,000 works. The periods of modern art represented include: '40s to '60s, '60s to '70s, and contemporary. Primarily Catalan and Spanish art is exhibited with representation by some International artists. The museum hosts revolving temporary exhibitions, a cinema, concerts and other cultural events.

Barcelona has many museums celebrating the artists of Spain. The museum of the **Fundació Joan Miró** exhibits works of the artist Joan Miró but also features guest exhibitions from other museums from around the globe. The **Picasso Museum** houses early works by Pablo Picasso and his Las Meninas series. The **Fundació Antoni Tàpies** holds a collection of Tàpies works.

The Museu Marítim de Barcelona, located in the historical Barcelona Royal Shipyard complex, is a nautical museum celebrating the Catalan seafaring culture and maritime history. **CosmoCaixa**, formerly the Science Museum, is one of the most exciting and largest museums in Barcelona with the exhibits arranged in levels around a huge tree and includes a rain forest, aquarium, geological and biological exhibits and a planetarium. **The Erotic Museum of Barcelona**, erotic art through the eyes of the great masters of painting, houses over 800 pieces of work including various cultures and religions. (It's an expensive tourist trap, so avoid it.)

ARCHITECTURE

The architecture of Barcelona reflects the city's 2000 years of history, some dating back to the time of the Romans with many great examples from the Gothic period and the Catalan art nouveau (el Modernisme) as well as the many magnificent modern buildings. Many of the buildings of Barcelona are well-known landmarks and popular tourist attractions. Topping the must-see list is the famous **Basilica Sagrada Familia**, the church known as the life's work of the famous architect **Antoni Gaudi**. (A friend of mind on his first visit likened it to "a Betty Crocker cake somebody put in a microwave and left in too long.")

Casa Milà (La Pedrera), also tops the list and visitors are fascinated with this quarry house with no right angles. One of the most beautiful Gothic buildings in Barcelona is the cathedral (**La Seu**) of Barcelona located in the middle of the Gothic Quarter with a magnificent Gothic interior. **Casa Batlló**, another creation of Gaudi, is

remembered for the roof that is arched like the back of a dragon. A visit to Barcelona is not complete without a stop at **Santa Maria del Mar**, another beautiful Gothic church that is one of the city's landmarks. Built in the early 14th century, the **Monastery of Pedralbes**, a beautiful example of Catalan gothic, offers beautiful gardens and a monastery museum. Located just steps off Las Ramblas, **the Palau Güell**, one of Gaudi's early masterpieces, is one of the most magnificent buildings in the Art Nouveau style. The concert hall of the **Palau de la Música** is filled with lots of glass, giving it a unique atmosphere and a reflection of both Modernism and Catalan Art Nouveau. Also not to be missed, **the Gran Teatre del Liceu** – home to performers such as Domingo, Pavarotti, Caballé, Callas and Tebaldi, is one of the most important opera houses in Europe and one of the most beautiful buildings in Barcelona. The **"Arc de Triumph"** built as the entrance to the World Exposition in 1888 was also erected as an homage to Picasso.

GETTING AROUND

Barcelona is a walkable city, especially through the main districts. Public transit offers an extensive network of buses, subway trains, trams, and local commuter rail. For schedules and a complete overview, check out the website of Transports Metropolitans de Barcelona (www.tmb.cat).

While they say driving in Barcelona in not dangerous, Spain has one of the highest traffic accident rates in Europe so it's safer to walk and use public transportation. I find it scarier than any other city, even Rome, and hold on for dear life when I'm in a cab. I think it has to do with the extremely narrow streets. The drivers barrel down them quite casually, however, and very fast. No jaywalking. Always look before crossing a street.

The A to Z Listings
Ridiculously Extravagant
Sensible Alternatives
Quality Bargain Spots

ABAC RESTAURANT
ABaC Hotel
Avenida Tibidabo 1, Barcelona, 34 933 19 66 00
http://www.abacbarcelona.com
CUISINE: Mediterranean, Spanish; Neo-Catalan
DRINKS: Full Bar

SERVING: Breakfast/Brunch, Lunch, & Dinner
PRICE RANGE: $$$$
NEIGHBORHOOD: Sarriá – Sant Gervasi
The prices were astronomical even before Chef Jordi
Cruz bagged the second of his Michelin stars. It's
always been popular as a power-lunch spot, but now
it's always packed. The place only seats about 55 or
60 people, so it might be a good idea to come for a
late breakfast (it's in a hotel a little out of the center
of town, so has to serve breakfast) if you're pushed
for time. They offer a couple of prix-fixe menus.
With the raw Hamachi, you'll get cherries and
cucumber "snow." Sweet corn taco with foie gras;
spider crab and caviar with chili oil. Iberian pork
meatballs; saffron and orange-infused prawn
bouillabaisse. The desserts are even more complex
than the other small plates. I can't imagine coming to
work here if you had a headache. The chefs are like
auto mechanics, not cooks. It's as if they need a Ph.D
to boil water.

ALKIMIA
Ronda Sant Antoni, 41, Barcelona, 34 932 07 61 15
http://www.alkimia.cat
CUISINE: Catalan / Spanish
DRINKS: Beer & Wine
SERVING: Lunch & Dinner (Closed Saturdays)
PRICE RANGE: $$$
NEIGHBORHOOD: L'Eixample
Offbeat twists on traditional Catalan dishes are what
you can expect to find in this very "smart" restaurant
situated in an old repurposed beer factory, but in a
room that's been completely modernized. That's not

the only surprising thing about this place, where they serve Michelin level food. Try any of the delicious seafood entrées (that's the chef's specialty—I like the langoustine with peppers). For something really different, get the gizzards with Campari and pickles. I grew up eating chicken gizzards in South Carolina, but, wow, they never tasted *this* good!

ANGLE
Carrer Aragón, 214, Barcelona, 34 932 167 777
www.anglebarcelona.com
CUISINE: Spanish, Catalan
DRINKS: Full Bar
SERVING: Lunch & Dinner
PRICE RANGE: $$$$
NEIGHBORHOOD: L'Eixample
Located in the Cram Hotel, this eatery is one of the high-profile spots in Barcelona. Favorites: Cod with mascarpone and almonds and Roast guinea fowl with foie, eggplant and black garlic. Impressive wine list. Popular brunch destination. Total upscale experience.

ASSUNTA MADRE
300 Carrer de Provenza, Barcelona, +34 932 15 32 35
www.assuntabarcellona.es
CUISINE: Italian/Seafood/Mediterranean
DRINKS: Full Bar
SERVING: Lunch & Dinner
PRICE RANGE: $$
NEIGHBORHOOD: Eixample District
This place is known for fresh fish. With the exposed red brick walls, the white tablecloths, you'll feel like you're going into an old-style Italian restaurant still

pretending to be on the formal side when it's a little past its prime. If you're sick of tapas you've had everywhere else, come here for a break. But get a pasta with seafood in it. Daily specials are always a winner (but double-check the price). Favorites: Sea Bass and Red Tuna. No meat on the menu. Vegetarian, Vegan and Gluten-free options.

AURT
Passeig del Taulat, 262, Barcelona, +34 935 07 08 60
https://www.aurtrestaurant.com/en
CUISINE: Spanish/Fusion
DRINKS: Wine
SERVING: Lunch & Dinner
PRICE RANGE: $$$
NEIGHBORHOOD: L'Eixample District
Unique eatery located inside the lobby of the **Hilton Diagonal Mar** hotel offering a tasting-menu-only of exotic small plates in a very intimate setting where you sit just a few feet from the chefs working on the

food. Menu is always changing in a place like this. Michelin level food but in an ultra-casual setting. Foodie types are known to frequent this place. (And for good reason.) Favorites: Sea Urchins and Cuttlefish tagliatelle. Nice wine pairings.

BACOA
Avinguda del Marquès de I'Argentera, 1, Barcelona, 34 933 107 313
www.bacoa.es
CUISINE: Burgers
DRINKS: Beer & Wine
SERVING: Lunch & Dinner
PRICE RANGE: $
NEIGHBORHOOD: Sant Pere, Santa Caterina i la Ribera
Normally you don't travel to Spain to order a burger but the burgers here are top-notch all made to order. Order a plain cheeseburger or one with fixins' like avocado, grilled onions, black beans, and their special mayo sauce. Order and pay at cash register but it's so popular you can wait up to 45 minutes to order.

BALUARD BAKERY

Carrer de Baluard 38-40, Barcelona, 34 932 211 208
http://baluardbarceloneta.com/en/principal
CUISINE: Bakery
DRINKS: No Alcohol
SERVING: All Day
PRICE RANGE: $
NEIGHBORHOOD: Barceloneta
Local bakery that supplies many of the high-end restaurants in town with breads and baked goods so you know it's good. Great selection of fresh baked breads, baguettes, fruit tarts, cannolis and other specialties.

BAR CAÑETE
Carrer de la Unió, 17, Barcelona, +34 932 70 34 58
www.barcanete.com
CUISINE: Spanish / Mediterranean / Tapas
DRINKS: Full Bar
SERVING: Lunch, Dinner, Late Night
PRICE RANGE: $$$
NEIGHBORHOOD: El Raval
Catalonian-style eatery offering a creative menu in a
raucous place that's always busy, loud, fun and
bustling. (This is not a quiet date night place, far from
it.) It has a big reputation, and deservedly so. Because
it's in all the guidebooks, it's packed with tourists,
but if you go late when the locals have dinner (no
earlier than 10 pm), you'll find the crowd has
suddenly become 100% local. I stay away from the

big meals here and focus on the tapas—mainly because I know the quality of the ingredients here cannot be surpassed by any other restaurants in Barcelona serving tapas—so order lots of little plates – baby squid, razor clams, burrata & tomatoes & pesto; Santa Pau beans in a stew; and Suckling Iberian Pig. Hell, order anything on this menu. It's that good. Try things you've never heard of. This is one of those places where I advise you to be adventurous. Vegan and Gluten-free options.

BAR JAI-CA
Carrer de Ginebra, 13, Barcelona, 34 932 683 265
www.barjaica.com
CUISINE: Tapas Bars
DRINKS: Full bar
SERVING: Breakfast, Lunch & Dinner; closed Monday
PRICE RANGE: $$
NEIGHBORHOOD: Barceloneta
Small restaurant that's usually packed but the turnover is quick. Nice variety of tapas including: patatas bravas, meatballs and deep-fried cuttlefish. No English spoken here.

BAR LOBO
Pintor Fortuny 3, Barcelona, 34 934 81 5346
https://grupotragaluz.com/restaurante/bar-lobo//
CUISINE: Bar, Tapas
DRINKS: Full Bar
SERVING: Breakfast, Lunch, Dinner & Late Night
PRICE RANGE: $$
NEIGHBORHOOD: El Raval
Trendy, modern restaurant located off the beaten
path. Great selection of food served tapas style.
Delicious dishes like Hummus, tomato and
mozzarella and tandoori chicken. Ideal choice for
breakfast.

BAR MUT
Calle Pau Claris, 192, Barcelona, 34 932 174 338
http://www.barmut.com
CUISINE: Wine Bar, Tapas/Small Plates
DRINKS: Full Bar
SERVING: Lunch, Dinner & Late Night

PRICE RANGE: $$$$
NEIGHBORHOOD: L'Eixample
Cozy modern restaurant that's perfect for a romantic
date. Small menu features selection of seafood and
tapas. Menu picks: Egg carpaccio and Grilled
octopus. Nice list of Spanish wines.

BAR PINOTXO
Rambla 91, Mercat de Boqueria, Barcelona, 34 933
171 731
http://www.pinotxobar.com
CUISINE: Tapas, Bar
DRINKS: Beer & Wine
SERVING: Breakfast, Brunch & Lunch
PRICE RANGE: $$
NEIGHBORHOOD: El Raval

Small tapas bar known for fish dishes. Seats about 12. Tapas selections include: Chickpeas, Razor clams, and Shrimp. Excellent espresso.

BAR VELODROMO
Carrer de Muntaner, 213, Barcelona, 34 934 306 022
http://www.moritz.cat
CUISINE: Tapas, Small Plates
DRINKS: Full Bar
SERVING: Lunch & Dinner
PRICE RANGE: $$
NEIGHBORHOOD: L'Eixample:
Located in a restored Art Deco building, this spacious eatery offers a varied assortment of Barcelona basics – eggs, tapas, churros dipped in chocolate, pastries, sausages and coffees. Favorites: Veggie pasta dish and Eggplant with basil mozzarella. Delicious café con leche.

BAR DEL PLA
Carrer Montcada, Num. 2, Barcelona, 34 932 68 30 03
http://www.bardelpla.cat
CUISINE: Mediterranean, Tapas
DRINKS: Beer & Wine
SERVING: Breakfast, Brunch & Late Night
PRICE RANGE: $$$
NEIGHBORHOOD: Barri Gòtic
Great authentic eatery featuring super tapas. Favorites: Tuna tartar and Mushrooms & strawberries. Excellent desserts. Craft beer. Reservations recommended.

BARRACA
Passeig Maritim de la Barceloneta 1, Barcelona, 34
93 224 12 53
barraca-barcelona.com.
CUISINE: Mediterranean
DRINKS: Full bar
SERVING: Lunch/Dinner/Late Night
PRICE RANGE: $$$
NEIGHBORHOOD: East End
Located on the beachfront, this nice restaurant offers
some of the best paella and fish you'll find in
Barcelona. Menu features traditional recipes of
Catalan gastronomy. Sidewalk tables and inside
dining on the second floor with a view of the water.

BEACH HOUSE
Carrer del Judici, 15, Barcelona, 34 932 211 658
No Website
CUISINE: Modern European
DRINKS: Full bar
SERVING: Breakfast, Lunch/Dinner
PRICE RANGE: $
NEIGHBORHOOD: Barceloneta
Close to the beach, this place offers terrace dining.
Great burgers and Chicken fillet sandwiches. The
cocktails are pricey but worth it.

BENZINA

Passatge de Pere Calders, 6, Barcelona, +34 936 59
55 83
www.benzina.es
CUISINE: Italian
DRINKS: Full Bar
SERVING: Dinner Wed – Fri & Sun, Lunch on Sat &
Sun; Closed Mon & Tues
PRICE RANGE: $$$
NEIGHBORHOOD: L'Eixample
Located in a former auto repair shop, this eatery
serves Italian fare in a romantic atmosphere, but it
still has a lovely bar crowd that gathers here before
heading elsewhere for dinner. It's Italian cuisine on
the "comfort food" side of the scale. Favorites:
Carbonara bursting with the flavor of eggs; Linguini
with lobster, garlic, oil; Spinach & cheese ravioli with
salmon tartare and Octopus & Pecorino. Creative
cocktails.

BICNIC
Carrer de Girona, 68, Barcelona, +34 690 90 46 14
www.bicnic.com
CUISINE: Catalan/Mediterranean
DRINKS: Full Bar
SERVING: Lunch & Dinner
PRICE RANGE: $$
NEIGHBORHOOD: L'Eixample
Billed as "gastro rustic" cuisine, this eatery offers unique twists on familiar Catalan dishes. They started in a food truck, and morphed into this clean, sleek, modern room that's very popular with locals. They have a menu that's divided into 2 sections, FAST and SLOW, depending on how fast you want to get in and get out. (Never seen that before.) I've tried both, and both are good, but if you have the time, go SLOW— far more fun. Favorites: Beef & eel tartare over roasted bone marrow (sinfully delicious); Monkfish with onions; and the excellent Codfish. Vegetarian friendly. Nice wine selection.

BOCA CHICA
Passatge de la Concepcion No. 12, First Floor, Barcelona, 34 934 67 51 49
http://www.bocagrande.cat
CUISINE: Spanish
DRINKS: Full Bar
SERVING: Late Night
PRICE RANGE: $$$
NEIGHBORHOOD: Catalonia

Two level chic restaurant/bar. Dinner downstairs but upstairs the elegant bar offers an extensive menu of classical, creative cocktails. Food is also good with a varied menu of dishes like Burrata salad and Pulpo.

BOCA GRANDE
Passatge de la Concepció, 12, Barcelona, 34 934 675 149
www.bocagrande.cat/en/
CUISINE: Catalan
DRINKS: Full bar
SERVING: Lunch/Dinner/Late Night
PRICE RANGE: $$$
NEIGHBORHOOD: L'Eixample
Upscale, trendy seafood eatery is a locals' favorite. Menu picks: Mussels with French fries and Black spaghetti with seafood. Reservations recommended. Before you leave check out the unisex bathrooms in the basement. (There's even a DJ down there!) Don't forget dessert – they are incredible here, especially the chocolate Tiramisu.

BODEGA 1900
Carrer de Tamarit, 91, Barcelona, 34 933 252 659
www.bodega1900.com/en
CUISINE: Tapas/Wine Bar
DRINKS: Full bar
SERVING: Lunch/Dinner; closed Sunday & Monday
PRICE RANGE: $$
NEIGHBORHOOD: L'Eixample
Fast paced and lively tapas bar. Great Chef's menu
with specials like fried peppers, eggplant, and squid.
Flavors are typical of this type of eatery but the
vermouth adds a special kick. Inside and sidewalk
dining.

CA L'ESTEVET

Carrer de Valldonzella, 46, Barcelona, +34 933 01 29 39

www.restaurantestevet.com

CUISINE: Spanish

DRINKS: Full Bar

SERVING: Lunch & Dinner (closed between lunch & dinner, 3:30 to 7), Lunch only on Sundays

PRICE RANGE: $$

NEIGHBORHOOD: El Raval

Catalan-style eatery featuring more of a home cooking approach, though the food is most carefully prepared. It's as if your grandmother was cooking instead of a Michelin chef. And that's quite fine with me, thank you very much. Extremely popular among the locals. The place dates back a hundred years, and you'd think they just installed those hideous harsh lights yesterday, but it doesn't matter. Vegetarian friendly. Hangout of celebrities and the local artistic community. I suggest you drink the same cheap local wine that they are drinking at the next table. That's what I do when I come here, and I never come to Barcelona without popping in here. Favorites: Cod fritters; Seafood Paella; Cuttlefish; Prawns; and Beef tenderloin.

CA L'ISIDRE
Carrer de les Flors, 12, Barcelona, 34 934 411 139
http://www.calisidre.com/
CUISINE: Seafood, Catalan, Mediterranean
DRINKS: Full Bar
SERVING: Lunch & Dinner (Closed Sundays)
PRICE RANGE: $$$$
NEIGHBORHOOD: El Raval
Family owned restaurant offering traditional Mediterranean cuisine. Simple menu with variety of choices from meat to seafood, even goat. Great selection of cheeses. Impressive wine list. Delicious desserts especially the chocolate soufflé – Woody Allen's favorite chocolate in Barcelona.

CAL PEP
Plaça de les Olles, 8, Barcelona, 34 933 10 79 61
http://www.calpep.com
CUISINE: Mediterranean, Tapas Bar
DRINKS: Full Bar
SERVING: Lunch & Dinner
PRICE RANGE: $$
NEIGHBORHOOD: Sant Pere, Santa Caterina i la Ribera
Very popular tapas bar (reservations are permitted only for parties of four or more). Menu favorites: Fried calamari, spinach with chickpeas (this is really

good) and little prawns. Ask the waiters for the daily specials. (They don't usually offer to tell you, so you have to ask them.) The chef chooses what you get depending on the number in your party and what you like or dislike. Expect to wait an hour for a table if you can't put together a party of 4.

CAN MAÑO
Almirall Aixada nº23, Barcelona, 93 221 54 55
www.canmajo.es/
CUISINE: Catalan
DRINKS: Full Bar
SERVING: Lunch & Dinner
PRICE RANGE: $$
NEIGHBORHOOD: Barceloneta
Nothing fancy here except the lip-smacking food enjoyed by the locals. Fried artichokes, calamari, grilled prawns, grilled cuttlefish, absolutely the freshest seafood available in town (at half the price at

the touristy places). They don't speak English, but they have a menu printed in English. But I'd say pretty much anything you order here will be a thorough delight. (A friend who lives a few blocks away brought me here the first time—now I go back every trip I make to Barcelona.)

CASA CALVET
Carrer de Casp, 48, Barcelona, 34 934 124 012
http://www.casacalvet.es
CUISINE: Spanish, Catalan
DRINKS: Full Bar
SERVING: Lunch & Dinner
PRICE RANGE: $$$$
NEIGHBORHOOD: L'Eixample
Located in an Antoni Gaudi building, Chef Miquel Alija offers a creative menu of creative Mediterranean cuisine. Menu picks: Spider crab croquettes and Pistachio-crusted lamb chops. Nice selection of wines. Great desserts. One of the highlights of Barcelona.

CASA GISPERT
Sombrerers 23, Barcelona, 34 93 319 75 35
www.casagispert.com
NEIGHBORHOOD: Sant Pere
Cute little shop (been here since 1851) located in the old section of Barcelona. This shop specializes in nuts (almonds, walnuts, pecans) and they use a 150-year old roaster. Buy nuts by weight but they also sell prepacked bags of nuts and staples like figs, beans (all types), lentils, and saffron. English is limited.

CASA LEOPOLDO

Carrer de Sant Rafael, 24, Barcelona, +34 934 413 014

www.casaleopoldo.com
CUISINE: Tapas bar / Catalonian
DRINKS: Full Bar
SERVING: Lunch & Dinner, Lunch only on Sundays
PRICE RANGE: $$
NEIGHBORHOOD: El Raval

Historic eatery known as a meeting spot for painters and writers (though it was a LOT less expensive when those "painters and writers" met here than it is now). Originally opened in 1929, it went through a big refurbishment and reopened in 2018 as a much more modern spot. But the tiled walls, the posters of bullfighters and prints & paintings of famous artists of the past—all that is still here. Though locals still come here, this area is quite touristy now, so there is a mix. However, a lot of the restaurants in this area serve sub-par food (catering to tourists who don't know any better.) Not so here. Menu (changes often) of small dishes and tapas to share. My Favorites: Oxtail in red wine; Anchovies in olive oil.

CEVICHE 103

Carrer de Londres, 103, Barcelona, 34 932 09 88 35
http://www.ceviche103.com
CUISINE: Peruvian
DRINKS: Full Bar
SERVING: Lunch & Late Night
PRICE RANGE: $$$$
NEIGHBORHOOD: L'Eixample

Modern, cozy eatery offering a creative menu of Peruvian cuisine specializing in ceviche. Menu picks: Ceviche of wild sea bass and King prawn tower with yellow pepper Aioli.

CINC SENTIS
Carrer d'Entença, 60, Barcelona, +34 933 23 94 90
www.cincsentits.com
CUISINE: Catalan/Modern European
DRINKS: Full Bar
SERVING: Lunch & Dinner; Closed Sun & Mon
PRICE RANGE: $$$$
NEIGHBORHOOD: L'Eixample
Upscale Michelin eatery in a stark modern formal setting—feels a little like church or a high end jewelry store when you come in here. Serious. Solemn. Go for the larger tasting menu with wine pairings. Favorites: Calamari (like you've never had it before, I promise you), with little piles of black

garlic—out of this world; Oven roasted Maitakehe; Aged "vaca vieja" beef. A real dining experience, even if it's a little boring.

COMERÇ 24
Carrer del Comerç, 24, Barcelona, 34 933 192 102
No Website
CUISINE: Mediterranean/Tapas
DRINKS: Full bar
SERVING: Lunch/Dinner; closed Sunday & Monday
PRICE RANGE: $$$$
NEIGHBORHOOD: Sant Pere
Popular upscale tapas bar (reservations needed—ask your concierge to do it for you). Typical Catalan ingredients with Asian and Latin preparations. Menu highlights: Tuna tartare and Duck rice with foie. Amazing wine list.

DISFRUTAR

Carrer de Villarroel, 163, Barcelona, +34 933 48 68 96

www.disfrutarbarcelona.com

CUISINE: Modern European/Mediterranean
DRINKS: Full Bar
SERVING: Lunch & Dinner
PRICE RANGE: $$$$
NEIGHBORHOOD: L'Eixample

Upscale 2-star Michelin eatery (featuring chefs from the late lamented El Bulli) offering four different highly creative dining options including tasting menus. The room is bright, light, casual—almost like an outdoor patio, even down to the furniture, with chairs with a webbed backing that look like they belong around a pool. In lieu of art on the walls, they've got a few recessed planter boxes up on the walls that are sleek, modern, fun. The wines are surprisingly cheap for a place like this, so splurge. There's a little outdoor seating area. Favorites: Panchino filled with beluga caviar and Razor clams with seaweed in salt. Dining takes several hours. Reservations necessary.

DOS PALILLOS

Carrer d'Elisabets, 9, Barcelona, 34 933 04 05 13

http://www.dospalillos.com

CUISINE: Spanish-Japanese Fusion
DRINKS: Full Bar
SERVING: Lunch & Dinner (closed Sun & Mon)
PRICE RANGE: $$$
NEIGHBORHOOD: El Raval

Though the chef is known for his hifalutin Michelin star level of food, this place is not stuffy and formal (like so many of those Michelin places where you feel more like you're in a church than a restaurant), but casual and fun. You sit at one of the couple of dozen stools at a counter bar surrounding the kitchen. Offers a traditional Spanish tapas-type bar, but with some surprising Asian twists that make this place unique (and in Barcelona, that's saying something). Order *a la carte* or from the tasting menu. (I always go with the tasting menu because there are so many surprises on it.) Menu picks: Cantonese Iberian pork belly; Jellyfish served Szechuan style; and the incredible Seabass. Creative desserts like Green tea ice cream in a sponge cake. Outdoor area as well. (By the way, the name means "two chopsticks" in Spanish.)

DRY MARTINI
Carrer d'Aribau, 162, Barcelona, 34 932 175 072
http://www.drymartinibcn.com

CUISINE: Bar
DRINKS: Full Bar
SERVING: 1:30 p.m. – 2:30 a.m.
PRICE RANGE: $$$
NEIGHBORHOOD: L'Eixample
An icon in the world of cocktails as it's the only
Spanish inclusion on the list of the 50 best bars in the
world and in Europe considered the third best bar.
The waiters and bartenders all wear tuxedos and they
are all pros. Here you'll find the perfect martini.
Every round comes with a different bar snack. You'll
find it to be pricier than most bars in Barcelona.
Friends I took there mentioned this, but later, this was
the bar they best remembered because it was so
damned stylish and classy.

ECLIPSE BAR
W Hotel, Plaça de la Rosa dels Vents 1, Barcelona,
34 93 295 2800
eclipse-barcelona.com.
CUISINE: Bar
DRINKS: Full bar
SERVING: Dinner/Late Night
PRICE RANGE: $$$
NEIGHBORHOOD: East End
Located on the 26th floor, this is the Barcelona branch
of the popular London bar. Incredible cocktails like
the famous Watermelon Martini and the Pink Floyd.
Sushi served before 11 p.m. Breathtaking view. Club
scene very exclusive.

EL CELLER DE CAN ROCA
Calle Can Sunyer, 48, Gerona, 34 972 222 157

http://www.cellercanroca.com
CUISINE: Spanish
DRINKS: Full Bar
SERVING: Breakfast, Brunch, lunch, Dinner & Late
Night
PRICE RANGE: $$$$
NEIGHBORHOOD: Cataluña
Reservations are at a premium here and usually made
up to 11 months in advance. But it's worth it. Great
menu with wine pairings. The Festival menu with
wine pairing featured over 19 courses with 17
different wines. This is a fine dining experience and
dinner usually takes about 4 hours.

EL QUIM DE LA BOQUERIA
Mercado de La Boqueria, La Rambla, 91, Barcelona,
34 933 019 810
elquimdelaboqueria.com
CUISINE: Spanish/Tapas
DRINKS: Beer & Wine
SERVING: Lunch
PRICE RANGE: $$
NEIGHBORHOOD: El Raval
Hidden gem located in Boqueria market, this bar style
eatery offers a creative menu of Spanish cuisine and
tapas. Menu picks: Fried artichoke and Eggs with
baby squid – their signature dish. Try the seafood
sampler.

EL MOLINO
Carrer de Vila i Vilà , 99, Barcelona, 34 932 055 111
http://www.elmolinobcn.com
CUISINE: Cabaret

DRINKS: Full Bar
SERVING: Late Night
PRICE RANGE: $
NEIGHBORHOOD: El Poble sec
Spanish cabaret featuring singing, dancing, and burlesque-style shows with acrobats hanging from the ceiling. Here you'll dance and have a great time.

EL VASO DE ORO
Calle de Balboa, 6, Barcelona, 34 933 193 098
www.vasodeoro.com
CUISINE: Spanish, Tapas
DRINKS: Full Bar
SERVING: Lunch & Dinner
PRICE RANGE: $
NEIGHBORHOOD: Barceloneta
Located off the beaten path, this local's favorite offers a simple menu (English and Spanish available). Menu picks: Steak with green peppers and their specialty – Russian salad.

EL XAMPANYET
Carrer de Montcada, 22, Barcelona, 34 933 19 70 03
http://www.guiatapear.com/tapas-barcelona/barcelona/item/el-xampanyet
CUISINE: Tapas Bar
DRINKS: Beer & Wine
SERVING: Dinner Closed Sunday & Monday
PRICE RANGE: $$
NEIGHBORHOOD: Sant Pere, Santa Caterina i la Ribera:
Small tapas bar with a large selection including many vegetarian options. Favorites: Artichokes, Red

peppers stuffed with cheese, and Sardines on toast. Cava flows freely here. Fun crowd with lots of regulars.

ENIGMA
Carrer de Sepúlveda, 38-40, Barcelona, 34 931 42 66 38
https://elbarri.com/restaurant/enigma/
CUISINE: Italian, Catalan
DRINKS: Beer & Wine
SERVING: Lunch & Dinner (Closed Saturdays & Sundays)
PRICE RANGE: $$$$$$$ (how many can I add?)
NEIGHBORHOOD: L'Eixample
A unique eatery offering a tasting menu only featuring over 40 courses (all right, they are tiny, but to get through so many, they'd have to be, right?) with an international flair. You never know what's on the menu, but there's always a little bit of everything. The chef here worked as pastry chef for 23 years in the famous El Bulli that closed in 2011. The same pretentious attitude is on display here, but so is the brilliance of the food. Guests need a secret code to enter the restaurant and need to pay a fee online to secure their reservation. Meals here usually last two-and-a-half to three hours. (Last time I ended up reading a book on my iPhone.) Seating is limited and the décor is quite whimsical with a selection of distinctly designed rooms. Food is the focus of this restaurant, so the wine list is limited. (What kind of excuse is that?)

ESCRIBÀ

Rambla de les Flors, 83, Barcelona, 34 933 016 027
www.escriba.es
CUISINE: Bakery
DRINKS: No Booze
SERVING: Lunch/Dinner
PRICE RANGE: $$
NEIGHBORHOOD: Barri Gòtic
Small but popular bakery. Try the hot chocolate –
almost pure chocolate. Great selection of pastries and
desserts. Amazing cheesecake. Breakfast options
include waffles with whipped cream.

ESPAI SUCRE

Carrer de la Princesa, 53, Barcelona, 34 932 681 630
http://www.espaisucre.com
CUISINE: Desserts
DRINKS: No Alcohol
SERVING: All Day
PRICE RANGE: $$$

NEIGHBORHOOD: Sant Pere, Santa Caterina i la Ribera

First you have to knock so they'll unlock the door. The name means sugar space so they specialize in desserts. Here you'll get a choice of unique desserts with ingredients that include tanka nut, celery, vinegar, coffee and coconut. A treat for the taste buds.

ESTIMAR

Carrer de Sant Antoni dels Sombrerers, 3, Barcelona, +34 679 36 39 15

www.restaurante-estimar.com

CUISINE: Seafood/ Spanish

DRINKS: Full Bar

SERVING: Lunch & Dinner

PRICE RANGE: $$$$

NEIGHBORHOOD: Sant Pere, Santa Caterina i la Ribera-Born

Attracting wealthier locals, this upscale eatery is known for fresh, intricately prepared seafood dishes—it's down a little alley, so you have to look out or you will pass it by. The seafood's the best you can get, and it will cost you. It will be displayed on a counter when you walk in. Though more than comfortable, this is not a "casual" evening out. The food quality elevates it to something more special than that. Favorites: Whole grilled sole; Baked John Dory and Langoustine carpaccio. Save room for the house-made Catalan cheesecake. Reservations recommended.

FABRICA MORITZ BARCELONA

Ronda de San Antoni, 39-41, Barcelona, 34 93 426 0050

http://www.moritz.com

CUISINE: Seafood, Tapas Bar, Beer Bar

DRINKS: Full Bar

SERVING: Dinner & Late Night

PRICE RANGE: $$

NEIGHBORHOOD: L'Eixample

This is actually the Moritz factory divided into four areas: wine bar, bar where tapas and their craft beer is served, waiting area and the store selling items related to beer. Menu features great seafood and tapas.

FEDERAL CAFÉ

Carrer del Parlament, 39, Barcelona, 34 931 873 607

http://www.federalcafe.es/barcelona

CUISINE: Brunch/ Burgers

DRINKS: Beer & Wine

SERVING: Brunch & Lunch

PRICE RANGE: $$

NEIGHBORHOOD: L'Eixample

Popular hip spot for brunch. Great breakfast selections like French toast with pears and Avocado toast. Fresh squeezed juices. Vegetarian options. Most of the staff speak English.

FERMI PUIG

Carrer Balmes, 175, Barcelona, 34 936 24 18 35

www.restaurantfermipuig.com

CUISINE: Mediterranean/Spanish

DRINKS: Full Bar

SERVING: Lunch & Dinner, only Lunch on Mondays
PRICE RANGE: $$$$
NEIGHBORHOOD: L'Eixample
Elegant eatery offering a mix of classical Catalan cuisine with more modern twists. Favorites: Smoked salmon, kid goat loin, crispy skinned monkfish and Avocado Cannelloni. Impressive wine list.

FISMULER
Carrer del Rec Comtal, 17, Barcelona, +34 935 14 00 50
www.fismuler.com
in Hotel Rec

CUISINE: Spanish/Tapas
DRINKS: Full Bar
SERVING: Lunch & Dinner
PRICE RANGE: $$
NEIGHBORHOOD: Sant Pere, Santa Caterina i la Ribera-Born

Relaxed eatery offers a great dining experience from a trio of alums from the great El Bulli. Street tiles cover the floor, and the tables look like old butcher block cubes. The menu changes daily, and even have the date punched on it so you can see. Favorites: Truffled chicken wings with egg & sweet potato; Viennese escalope (dished up tableside) and Cockles Risotto. Nice list of Spanish wines. Late dining. Live music. Wonderfully exciting atmosphere. Allow 3 hours for dinner. (They've never been known to rush here in Barcelona. If you're lucky enough to live here for an extended period, you'll quickly see why. They live better than we do.)

FONDA GAIG

Carrer de Còrsega, 200, Barcelona, 34 934 532 020
http://www.restaurantgaig.com
CUISINE: Mediterranean, Catalan, Signature Cuisine
DRINKS: Beer & Wine
SERVING: Lunch & Dinner
PRICE RANGE: $$$
NEIGHBORHOOD: L'Eixample

Modern looking restaurant offering traditional Catalonian cuisine attracting mostly locals. Menu favorites include: Canneloni and Squid with artichoke cream sauce. Tasting menu or a la carte. Staff speak English. 5 star food and service.

FORMATGERIA LA SEU

Carrer de la Dagueria, 16, Barcelona, 34 934 126 548
http://www.formatgerialaseu.com
CUISINE: Cheese Shop
DRINKS: Wine
SERVING: All Day – Closed Sundays
PRICE RANGE: $$$
NEIGHBORHOOD: Barri Gòtic
Visit on a quiet day and owner Katherine McLaughlin
will delight you with stories about Catalan cheese. All
the cheeses are handpicked by the owner. Enjoy three
cheeses and a glass of wine.

GREEN SPOT

Carrer de la Reina Cristina, 12, Barcelona, +34 938
02 55 65
www.encompaniadelobos.com
CUISINE: Vegetarian
DRINKS: Full Bar
SERVING: Lunch & Dinner
PRICE RANGE: $$$
NEIGHBORHOOD: Sant Pere, Santa Caterina i la
Ribera-Born
Modern look with lots of wooden slatted walls,
butcher-block style tables in this upscale eatery
serving vegetarian fare that they claim is "veggie for
non-veggies." That is mostly true. A lot of young
trendy types stop here on their way to the beach—or
back from it. Favorites: Eggplant Calzone; Fried
cauliflower with mint and Pasta Madre. Vegetables
take center focus here. Reservations recommended.

GRESCA
Calle Provença, 230, Barcelona, 34 934 516 193
http://www.gresca.net
WEBSITE DOWN AT PRESSTIME
CUISINE: Gastropub
DRINKS: Full Bar
SERVING: Lunch & Dinner; closed Sunday
PRICE RANGE: $$
NEIGHBORHOOD: L'Eixample
Interesting mix of French & Spanish cuisine in this
affordable place mostly frequented by locals. The
place doesn't jump out at you. I walked by it several
times before deciding to try it for lunch. Very
impressed. Menu picks: Egg soufflé; Veal

sweetbreads; and Gnocchi. Try their classic Tiramisu or unique Pear & Coffee for dessert.

GRANJA M. VIADER
Carrer Xuclà, 4-6, Barcelona, 34 933 18 3486
http://www.granjaviader.cat
CUISINE: Breakfast, Coffee & Tea
DRINKS: Beer & Wine
SERVING: Breakfast & Brunch; closed Sunday
PRICE RANGE: $
NEIGHBORHOOD: El Raval
Cozy café where you order at the counter delicious coffee and pastries. Favorites: Spanish hot chocolate and churros. Local's favorites.

HAWKER 45
Carrer de Casp, 45, Barcelona, +34 937 63 83 15
www.hawker45.com
CUISINE: Asian Fusion
DRINKS: Full Bar
SERVING: Lunch & Dinner, Lunch only on Sundays
PRICE RANGE: $$
NEIGHBORHOOD: L'Eixample
Creative offering of Asian Fusion cuisine in a simple room with a scarlet-topped bar with metal chair. A little austere, but clean and modern. Regular and tasting menus offered. Menu picks: Korean fried chicken wings (wonderful); Indian pancake with sautéed carrots; Rice Laksa from Singapore with shrimp and squid; and the Chicken Satay, very differently prepared from what I've seen elsewhere in the world. Save room for desserts (unusual and tasty).

Fantastic cocktails like the Vermouth pisco with coffee beans.

HOJA SANTA
Avinguda de Mistral, 54, Barcelona, 34 933 482 194
www.hojasanta.es/en
CUISINE: Mexican/Latin American
DRINKS: Full Bar
SERVING: Dinner (Closed Sundays & Mondays)
PRICE RANGE: $$$$
NEIGHBORHOOD: L'Eixample
Menu of authentic Mexican dishes influence by other cuisines. Try the tasting menu giving you an opportunity to try all their famous dishes. Favorites: Hoja leaf and Avocado gazpacho. Nice selection of cocktails.

IDEAL COCKTAIL BAR
Carrer d'Aribau, 89, Barcelona, 34 934 531 028
http://www.idealcocktailbar.com
CUISINE: Cocktail Bar
DRINKS: Full Bar
SERVING: 12:30 p.m. – 2: 30 a.m.
PRICE RANGE: $$
NEIGHBORHOOD: L'Eixample
Around since the '20s & '30s, this elegant bar is owned by the grandson of the original owner. Top notch cocktails and classic English style.

ISABELLA'S
Carrer de Ganduxer, 50, Barcelona, 34 934 145 769
http://www.isabellas-restaurant.com
CUISINE: Mediterranean, Italian

DRINKS: Full Bar
SERVING: Lunch & Dinner
PRICE RANGE: $$$
NEIGHBORHOOD: Sarrià – Sant Gervasi
Dining room decorated with a collection of eclectic furniture giving you the feel of dining in someone's home. Nice selection of local dishes, pastas and pizzas. Favorites: Steak tartare and Lemon Meringue tart. Outdoor terrace for dining weather permitting.

KOSKA TAVERNA
Carrer de Blai, 8, Barcelona, 34 931 270 313
http://www.koskataverna.com
CUISINE: Tapas
DRINKS: Full Bar
SERVING: Dinner & Late Night
PRICE RANGE: $$
NEIGHBORHOOD: El Poble-sec
Excellent tapas bar with 90% of the menu gluten-free with lots of vegetarian options. Though the quality of the cuisine can't be overrated, you'll find the rustic setting the definition of simplicity itself. Menu picks: Cow cheek tapas and the cheese sampler. Menu picks: Cow cheek tapas and the cheese sampler.

LA BARRA DE CARLES ABELLAN
Hotel W
Vela, Planta E, Barcelona, +34 932 95 26 36
www.carlesabellan.com
CUISINE: Seafood/Mediterranean
DRINKS: Full Bar
SERVING: Lunch & Dinner
PRICE RANGE: $$$$
NEIGHBORHOOD: Barceloneta
Located in Hotel W, this haute cuisine eatery
celebrates the famous Chef Carles and his exquisite
seafood (after, first and foremost, celebrating the hip
trendy stylish crowd the place attracts). There's a lot
of glitz and hype and glamor associated with this
place. There's even live footage of the kitchen on the
floor below visible on screens in the dining room.
(Why, I can't quite say. I think it's stupid.) This is *not*

a quiet night out, but rather a foray into one of the hippest places in town. Beyond the hype, however, the food certainly does measure up to the best you can get here in Barcelona. There's a sad lonely meat option on the menu, a highly prized Wagyu cut, but forget about it and revel in the seafood. This is one of those places that's hot, hot, hot—and also good, good, good. There's no faking it in the kitchen (as you can see for yourself on the screens above you). Favorite tapas: Garlic shrimp carpaccio; Pickled octopus and Fried oyster with salmon roe. Communal counter/tables. Gluten Free options.

LA BOQUERIA
La Rambla, 91, Barcelona, 34 933 18 25 84
Business website boqueria.info
www.boqueria.info
NEIGHBORHOOD: El Raval
A great experience is browsing through this popular market with stalls offering everything from fruits, spices, meats, cheeses, spices, and sea food. They also sell prepared food if you're hungry. Fresh juices from mango to dragon fruit. Cash only.

LA CLARA
Gran Via de les Corts Catalanes, 442, Barcelona, 34 932 893 460
www.laclararestaurant.com
CUISINE: Modern European/Spanish
DRINKS: Full bar
SERVING: Lunch/Dinner/Late Night
PRICE RANGE: $$$
NEIGHBORHOOD: L'Eixample

Upscale eatery offering a menu of local delicacies. Menu picks: Grilled veal, kidneys cooked with sherry and Mozzarella with pesto. Steaks served to perfection. Great desserts. Good selection of items for kids. Note: TVs playing soccer games loudly make conversation a little difficult here, but it's great fun.

LA COVA FUMADA
Carrer Baluard, 56, Barcelona, 34 932 214 061
No Website
CUISINE: Tapas
DRINKS: Full Bar
SERVING: Breakfast & Lunch; closed Sunday
PRICE RANGE: $$
NEIGHBORHOOD: Barceloneta
There's no sign outside but once inside you'll be welcomed (often by the owner). Nice selection of tapas, bombas and dishes like fried squid, grilled

calamaris, and fried codfish. Often a 30-minute wait to get inside.

LA DAMA
Avinguda Diagonal, 423, Barcelona, +34 932 096 328
http://www.la-dama.com/
CUISINE: Catalan/French
DRINKS: Full Bar
SERVING: Lunch & Dinner, Lunch only on Sat; Closed on Sundays
PRICE RANGE: $$$
NEIGHBORHOOD: L'Eixample
Located in a 'secret' apartment with a doorman greeting you as you enter the Belle Epoque mansion-like dining room setting, you'll feel like a guest of a wealthy aristocrat (and, by the way, an aristocrat who happens to be a great cook). The house, which dates

to 1917, was built by a student of the great Gaudi. Well worth getting there early so you can enjoy some excellent cocktails mixed by professional bartenders who know what they're doing. By coming in early, you'll get to spend more time taking in this stunning mansion, called **Casa Sayrach**. Expansive menu of Catalan and Spanish regional cuisine. Staff speaks multiple languages. Favorites: Braised pork; Squid ink carbonara and Steamed Sea Bass. Nice wine pairings. Flawless service.

LA GUINGUETA
Av. del Litoral, 62, Barcelona, 34 633 72 25 66
https://restaurantsescriba.com/laguinguetaescriba/
CUISINE: Mediterranean, Tapas
DRINKS: Beer & Wine
SERVING: 9:00 a.m. - Midnight
PRICE RANGE: $
NEIGHBORHOOD: Barceloneta
Beachside restaurant offering giant umbrellas, loungers, and beer. Simple menu of burgers and such. Kitchen is open for breakfast, tapas, and bar fare. Go for the grilled razor clams, cilantro ceviche, octopus grilled and sprinkled with pimento. Definitely get a side order of the excellent guacamole.

LA TAVERNA DEL CLINIC
Carrer del Rosselló, 155, Barcelona, +34 934 10 42 21
www.latavernadelclinic.com
CUISINE: Tapas bar
DRINKS: Full Bar

SERVING: Breakfast, Lunch, & Dinner; Closed
Sundays
PRICE RANGE: $$$$
NEIGHBORHOOD: L'Eixample
Upscale eatery (in terms of the food) in a nondescript
setting (in terms of the modestly old fashioned décor)
serving regional classics expertly made by an award-
winning young chef. You won't find many tourists
here. Rather, you'll see business people and well-
heeled locals who know what they're doing. My
Menu picks: Candied bacon with mashed potatoes
and Roasted duck. Impressive and carefully selected
wine list, with a much broader selection than most
places.

LLURITU
Carrer del Torrent de les Flors, 71, Barcelona, +34
938 55 38 66
www.lluritu.com
CUISINE: Seafood/Spanish
DRINKS: Full Bar
SERVING: Weird hours: Dinner Wed & Thursday
from 7; Friday, 1 pm to midnight; Sat & Sun, 11:30 to
midnight; Closed Monday and Tuesday – **check
website to be sure.**
PRICE RANGE: $$
NEIGHBORHOOD: Gràcia
Simple eatery offering a menu of seafood tapas to a
mainly locals crowd. Focus on shellfish dishes.
Favorites: Grilled sardines; Grilled squid; Steamed
clams. They have a big seafood platter that gives you
a bit of everything. Avoid those tedious tourist traps

on Las Ramblas and come here for the real thing.
Open kitchen. Reservations recommended.

LOLITA TAPERÍA
Carrer de Tamarit, 104, Barcelona, 34 934 245 231
http://www.lolitataperia.com
CUISINE: Bar, Tapas
DRINKS: Full Bar
SERVING: Dinner
PRICE RANGE: $$$
NEIGHBORHOOD: L'Eixample
A combination bar, vermouthery (on Saturdays at noon), restaurant and bistro. Extensive menu of traditional tapas and small snacks. Bar serves Spanish wines, cava, and Moritz beer. Outdoor terrace.

MAREA ALTA
Av. de les Drassanes, 6, Barcelona, +34 936 31 35 90
www.mareaaltamareabaja.com
CUISINE: Mediterranean/Seafood

DRINKS: Full Bar
SERVING: Lunch & Dinner
PRICE RANGE: $$$
NEIGHBORHOOD: El Raval
Perched atop the Torre Colom, one of the very few tall buildings in Barcelona, is this high-end restaurant that serves simply prepared, fresh seafood. Stunning 360-degree views of the waterfront and the entire city. Marea Alta takes up the entire floor, so views are unobstructed. Romantic setting. Good for special occasions. Dressy because it's special. I always go to the bar on the 23rd floor, **Marea Baja**, before *and* after dinner, when the vibe changes into more of a nightclub scene. Very slick and trendy. Order a whole fish (like Sea Bass or even better, the whole grilled Turbot or the Monkfish) to split with your guests. There are a lot of great seafood eateries in Barcelona, and though a handful may equal this place, I can't say they surpass it. In any way. (Plus, there's that view—you'll feel like you're on the bridge of an ocean liner.) Delicious desserts. Reservations recommended.

MARTINEZ
Ctra. de Miramar, 38, Barcelona, +34 931 06 60 52
www.martinezbarcelona.com
CUISINE: Mediterranean
DRINKS: Full Bar
SERVING: Lunch, Dinner, and Late Night
PRICE RANGE: $$$
NEIGHBORHOOD: Montjac
Upscale dining featuring breathtaking views from an outdoor deck that overlooks the city, the port and the

Mediterranean. Menu features dishes of fish, steak, chicken and ingredients from local markets. Paella is their specialty, and I definitely recommend it. (That being said, the monkfish and lobster rice are to die for.) For some reason, perched high above the expansive city, you end up taking longer at lunch here than you would anywhere else. It's just such a relaxing, removed feeling you get, as if the city rolling out below you were some kind of vision, not even real. Impressive cocktail selection.

MESON DEL CAFÉ
Carrer de la Libreria, 16, Barcelona, 34 933 150 754
No Website

CUISINE: Coffee & Tea, Tapas
DRINKS: Full Bar
SERVING: Breakfast, Lunch & Dinner: Closed
Sundays
PRICE RANGE: $$
NEIGHBORHOOD: Barri Gòtic
Small café with no menu – they will tell you what
they have. Not a tourist destination. Small selection
but the food is good and café con leches are the best.

MORRO FI
Carrer del Consell de Cent, 171, Barcelona
http://www.morrofi.cat
CUISINE: Tapas, Catalan, Mediterranean
DRINKS: Full Bar

SERVING: Lunch (Fri - Sun Only) & Dinner
PRICE RANGE: $ - **cash only**
NEIGHBORHOOD: L'Eixample
Small café (sits no more than 8 people) but it's popular for its Sweet Vermouth (Vermouth parties every Sunday). Small menu of tapas and small bites. Cash only.

MONVINIC
Carrer de la Diputaciò, 249, Barcelona, 34 932 726 187
http://www.monvinic.com/
CUISINE: Modern European, Catalan, Bar
DRINKS: Full Bar
SERVING: Lunch & Dinner; closed Sunday & Monday
PRICE RANGE: $$
NEIGHBORHOOD: L'Eixample
Great tapas bar but the real star is the wine. Excellent selection of wines including nice variety of local wines.

MUDANZAS
Vidrieria 15, Barcelona, 34-933-191-137
No Website
CUISINE: Bar Fare
DRINKS: Full Bar
SERVING: Lunch & Dinner
PRICE RANGE: $$
NEIGHBORHOOD: La Ribera / Born
Local hangout serving sandwiches and tapas. Basically bar fare.

OHLA BOUTIQUE BAR
Via Laietana, 49, Barcelona, 34 933 41 5050
www.ohlabarcelona.com/
CUISINE: Bar/Tapas
DRINKS: Full Bar
SERVING: Late Night
PRICE RANGE: $$$
NEIGHBORHOOD: Barri Gòtic
Bar serving creative cocktails and amazing tapas.
Menu picks: Pork tenderloin and Octopus on
potatoes. Live music some nights.

PACO MERALGO
Carrer de Muntaner, 171, Barcelona, +34 934 309
027
www.restaurantpacomeralgo.com
CUISINE: Tapas
DRINKS: Full Bar
SERVING: Lunch & Dinner Mon-Sat (closed from 4-
8 between lunch and dinner); closed Sunday.
PRICE RANGE: $$$
NEIGHBORHOOD: L'Eixample
Upscale eatery with a creative tapas menu. It's not so
much *what's* on the menu as how superior the
ingredients that go into what's on the menu that sets
this place apart from the hundreds of other tapas
joints in town. Serious foodies flock here because of
this quality. (Try to get a seat at the busy bar—much
more entertaining than at a table in the dining room.)
Favorites: "Obama" cuttlefish croquettes and Garlic
sizzling steak. Reservations necessary.

PAKTA

Calle Lerida, 5, Barcelona, 34 936 24 01 77

http://www.pakta.es

CUISINE: Asian Fusion, Peruvian

DRINKS: Full Bar

SERVING: Lunch (Sat Only) & Dinner (Tues to Sat)

PRICE RANGE: $$$$

NEIGHBORHOOD: El Poble-sec

This upscale modern Japanese-style eatery features a dining area and bar. Albert Adria of El Bulli fame was determined to offer the distinctive "Nikkei" cuisine that mixes Japanese and Peruvian styles. Only two tasting menu options here; a shorter Fujiyama course and a longer Machu Picchu course. Favorites: Pork jowl sandwich and Horse mackerel. Great Asian-inspired cocktails. It's very expensive, but quite unique.

PASSADIS DEL PEP

Pla de Palau, 2, Barcelona, +34 933 101 021

CUISINE: Mediterranean / Seafood / Catalan
DRINKS: Full Bar
SERVING: Lunch & Dinner; Closed Sundays
PRICE RANGE: $$$
NEIGHBORHOOD: Sant Pere, Santa Caterina i la Ribera-Born
Nondescript entrance (I think they do this on purpose), but once you find it, it's an unforgettable experience. A lot of celebrities have found it, so you can, too. There's a reason—it's simply great. And unique. Here they just start bringing you food (there's no menu to peruse) but for the main course, they will ask if you want meat or fish. (*Tip*—stick with the seafood.) They will ask you what you want and what your budget is, giving you the option basically to point them in the right direction. Manu changes daily based on what local ingredients they source. Creative cocktails and coffees. Big wine list, over 200 selections. This is a place you'll never forget, so do your best to come here. Good for families & friends

PARKING PIZZA
Carrer de Londres, 98, Barcelona, +34 936 339 645
www.parkingpizza.com
CUISINE: Pizza
DRINKS: Beer & Wine Only
SERVING: Lunch & Dinner; they close from 4 to 8 between Lunch & Dinner; Lunch only on Sundays.
Tip: if you're coming for dinner, get there early, by 8, or you'll have to wait in line. Turnover is fast, however.
PRICE RANGE: $$

NEIGHBORHOOD: L'Eixample
In a former car park is this vast hall with communal tables, the white lines marking the parking spaces still visible on the floor. Place is packed, with both locals and tourists in equal measure. Pizza, pizza, pizza. Wood-fired and served with a perfect crust. Many varieties (among 14) to select from including Buffalo mozzarella as well as the Margarita.

PEZ VELA
Passeig del Mare Nostrum 19-2, Barcelona, 34 932 216 317
grupotragaluz.com.
CUISINE: Spanish
DRINKS: Full bar
SERVING: Lunch/Dinner
PRICE RANGE: $$$
NEIGHBORHOOD: Barceloneta
Beach front eatery specializing on paellas, fresh appetizers and salads. Fresh seafood. Terrace offers

incredible views of the city and sea. A place to leisurely sit and enjoy your meal.

PICNIC
Carrer del Comerç, 1, Barcelona, +34 935 11 66 61
www.picnic-restaurant.com
CUISINE: Spanish / Mexican / Even some American
DRINKS: Full Bar
SERVING: Lunch & Dinner, Lunch only on Sun & Mon
PRICE RANGE: $$
NEIGHBORHOOD: Sant Pere, Santa Caterina i la Ribera-Born
Lots of menu options here (translated in English). Mexican based cuisine with tortillas, Huevo rancheros and tacos. A favorite Brunch spot. If you stop in for brunch, try the French toast served with apricot dressing; Quinoa hash browns (never had them before I had them here—outstanding); Pulled pork chilaquiles topped off with a poached egg & guac—now *this* is brunch. Seasonal menu based on what's available. Nice moderately priced wine selection. One of my favorite places in town.

QUIMET & QUIMET
Carrer del Poeta Cabanyes, 25, Barcelona, 34 934 42 31 42
https://www.quimetquimet.com/
CUISINE: Tapas Bar
DRINKS: Full Bar
SERVING: Lunch & Dinner; closed Sunday
PRICE RANGE: $$
NEIGHBORHOOD: El Poble-sec

Very tiny spot and it's usually standing room only. Be prepared to eat standing. Great assortment of tapas made right in front of you. Favorites: Artichoke and cheese with caviar and Salmon with yogurt. Vermouth on tap.

RED FISH
Moll de la Marina, s/n, Barcelona, +34 931 716 894
www.redfishbcn.com
CUISINE: Seafood/Spanish
DRINKS: Full Bar
SERVING: Lunch & Dinner
PRICE RANGE: $$$
NEIGHBORHOOD: La Vila Olímpica
It's right on the beach, which is nice. In fact, the expansive view of the water from its open-air outdoor seating area could not be improved upon. You get to see the whole vista of the waterfront. Most places in this part of town tend to be popular because they're on the beach, not because the food is any good. (All beach-front places confront the visitor with the same challenge—finding quality food in a casual resort atmosphere.) Here at Red Fish, however, the emphasis is firmly on the food. Has a menu of Spanish favorites served tapas-style. My Menu picks: the house specialty is superb—a Lobster Rice dish that's more like a rich soupy stew than a paella—just bursting with flavor. Chicken croquettes; Anchovies with extra salt. Excellent calamari.

RESTAURANT EMBAT
Carrer Mallorca, 304, Barcelona, 34 934 58 08 55
www.embatrestaurant.com

CUISINE: Spanish
DRINKS: Beer & Wine
SERVING: Lunch & Dinner; closed Sunday
PRICE RANGE: $$
NEIGHBORHOOD: L'Eixample
Nice comfortable restaurant with two options: 5 course tasting menu or order a la carte. Nice selection: Corn yogurt, anchovy salad, lamb, salmon, seafood risotto. Amazing desserts. Limited wine list.

RESTAURANTE SOMORROSTRO
Carrer de Sant Carles, 11, Barcelona, 34 932 250 010
www.restaurantesomorrostro.com
CUISINE: Seafood, Catalan
DRINKS: Full Bar
SERVING: Lunch & Dinner
PRICE RANGE: $$
NEIGHBORHOOD: Barceloneta
Comfortable eatery with tables that don't match and oddly shaped artwork on the walls. If you have to wait for a table, there's an amusement park a few blocks away where you can fill the time. They have a great menu with a strong focus on seafood. Their paella is famous. Reservations a must. Other favorites: Tuna tartare and Octopus with potatoes and chorizo. Try the Sangria, you'll probably order a second pitcher.

RÍAS DE GALICIA
Carrer de Lleida, 7, Barcelona, 34 934 248 152
www.riasdegalicia.com
CUISINE: Spanish/Seafood
DRINKS: Full bar
SERVING: Lunch/Dinner
PRICE RANGE: $$$$
NEIGHBORHOOD: El Poble-sec
Known as one of the best seafood restaurants in
Barcelona serving great dishes like: Mediterranean
Red Tuna Tartar, Octopus Galician style and their
specialty Blue Lobster.

ROIG ROBÍ
http://www.roigrobi.com
Carrer de Sèneca, 20, Barcelona, 34 932 189 222
CUISINE: Catalan, Mediterranean
DRINKS: Full Bar
SERVING: Lunch & Dinner; closed Sunday
PRICE RANGE: $$$
NEIGHBORHOOD: Grácia
Upscale Spanish eatery with great food. Order the
risotto – it's the best you'll ever eat. Other favorites:

Grilled octopus hummus and RR hake. Nice wine selection. Private patio in the back.

SAGÀS, PAGESOS, CUINERS & CO
Plà del Palau, 13, Barcelona, 34 933 102 434
http://www.sagaspagesosicuiners.com
CUISINE: Local Cuisine
DRINKS: Beer & Wine
SERVING: Breakfast, Brunch & Late Night
PRICE RANGE: $$
NEIGHBORHOOD: Sant Pere, Santa Caterina i la Ribera
Most of what you eat here will have originated from the farm owned by the wonderful chef, Oriol Rovira. But his vision is not so local. While the pigs may come from the farm close by, the menu selections come from around the world. Think Korean pork buns, homemade sausages that will send you reeling, black pudding, porchetta, everything to do with pork, but with excellent produce from the farm as well.

SHUNKA
Carrer de Sagristans, 5, Barcelona, 34 934 124 991

www.koyshunka.com
CUISINE: Japanese/Sushi
DRINKS: Full Bar
SERVING: Lunch Dinner & Late Night; closed
Monday
PRICE RANGE: $$$
NEIGHBORHOOD: Barri Gòtic
High end sushi and authentic Japanese restaurant. Not
your run of the mill Japanese eatery, tucked away on
a quiet street is the best Japanese restaurant in
Barcelona. Everything is fresh. Great selections: tajo
kimuchi, Kani maki, sake maki, toro tataki nigiri, and
ikura nigari. Reservations recommended.

SLOW & LOW
Carrer del Comte Borrell, 119, Barcelona, +34 936
254 512
www.slowandlowbcn.com
CUISINE: Spanish (though with a lot of touches from
diverse places such as Bali and Singapore, Mexico,
Peru)
DRINKS: Full Bar
SERVING: Lunch & Dinner; Closed Sun & Mon
PRICE RANGE: $$$
NEIGHBORHOOD: L'Eixample
Eclectic fine-dining eatery with an open kitchen. Try
to get one of the half dozen chairs at the kitchen bar.
This is one of those places that offers the highest level
of culinary experience in an atmosphere as laid back
as a Florida Keys oyster shack. Not that the place
looks like a Florida Keys oyster shack. Quite the
opposite. The tables here are hung from some
brackets in the ceiling and walls. The lighting is

careful, brilliantly executed. Very modern. Hip crowd. The kitchen crew are all trendier than you are—unless you sport a beard and have a lot of tats on your arms. Two tasting menus. No *a la carte* option. Small dishes with an emphasis on shellfish. Nice wine pairings.

SOLOMILLO
Carrer de Mallorca, 251, Barcelona, +34 934 677 755
www.restaurantesolomillo.com
CUISINE: Spanish/Steakhouse
DRINKS: Full Bar
SERVING: Breakfast, Lunch, & Dinner, Lunch only on Sundays; Closed Mondays
PRICE RANGE: $$$$
NEIGHBORHOOD: L'Eixample
Upscale eatery catering to steak lovers featuring spectacular cuts of sirloin. (The name "Solomillo" means "sirloin steak.") When you come in, you'll see a deli and a charcuterie bar laden with displays of cheeses. But if you go upstairs, you enter a different world—a bistro-style atmosphere with old-style lamps, leather upholstery, low lighting. Choose steak by weight. Gluten-free options, but who cares? One thing about the sides—be sure to get the dauphinois potatoes. Eye rollingly delicious. Extensive wine list—be sure to let your waiter guide you to a Spanish wine—they have really great Spanish reds represented handsomely on the wine card. Excellent desserts. Do not bring vegetarians here—you'll just ensure they have a miserable evening.

SPOONIK

Plaça de Lesseps, 13, Barcelona, +34 648 085 209
www.spoonik.com
CUISINE: Mediterranean / Latin America
DRINKS: Beer & Wine Only
SERVING: Dinner; Closed Mon – Thurs.
PRICE RANGE: $$$$
NEIGHBORHOOD: Gràcia
Beautifully designed restaurant offering a unique
dining experience that combines a lot of different
sensory elements—it's not just about the food. It's
performance art, with light shows, sound effects,
theatre, dancing, acrobatic performances by the
staff—all designed to give you an outer body
experience. This all happens in a secluded lushly

landscaped courtyard of a 19th Century private villa converted into a restaurant. The food—multi-course tasting menu with Catalan wine (and one beer) pairing. Unlike a lot of places that go overboard with antics designed to keep you from noticing the food, Spoonik only serves the very best quality of everything. The chef is a top award-winner, so you're in good hands. The avant-garde cabaret that you're in the midst of is simply refreshing and different. Creative dishes designed to mimic Spanish comfort food. Communal tables. Reservations/deposit necessary.

TAPAS 24
Carrer de la Disputacio, 269, Barcelona, 34 934 88 09 77
www.tapas24.ca
CUISINE: Tapas Bar
DRINKS: Full Bar
SERVING: Lunch & Dinner; closed Sunday
PRICE RANGE: $$
NEIGHBORHOOD: L'Eixample
Cute tapas bar with beer on tap and nice selection of house wines. Nice variety of tapas and desserts. Favorites: Bikini sandwiches and Steak. No reservations so expect a wait.

TICKETS BAR
Avinguda del Paral, 164, Barcelona, 34 932 924 252
http://www.ticketsbar.es
CUISINE: Tapas Bar, Spanish
DRINKS: Full Bar
SERVING: Dinner; closed Sunday & Monday
PRICE RANGE: $$$$
NEIGHBORHOOD: L'Eixample
The famed Ferran Adria did not rest on his laurels
after shutting down the iconic El Bulli. He and
brother Alberto opened this hot spot. It's tapas, yes,
but very sophisticated and high-minded: tuna belly
sliced so thin you can see through it; liquid olives
(yes, that's what I said); tempura made with algae.
This place is about as experimental as it gets. The
sorbets are made in-house and flavors change with the
season. I personally think they are more interested in
bending over backward to do something "new and
different" than they are in focusing on the food, but
nobody agrees with me. These guys are kind of the

Cirque du Soleil of the restaurant industry. You're paying for a show—you might as well get one. (Still, when I eat those crunchy tacos with the Chinese style suckling pig, I'm reminded that these guys are in the genius category.)

TLAXCAL
Carrer del Comerç, 27, Barcelona, 34 932 684 134
http://www.tlaxcal.com
CUISINE: Mexican
DRINKS: Full Bar
SERVING: Lunch & Dinner
PRICE RANGE: $$
NEIGHBORHOOD: Sant Pere, Santa Caterina i la Rivera-Born
Great authentic Mexican cuisine with an impressive selection of Mexican beers. Menu favorites: fish tacos, steak tacos, guacamole, and enchiladas.

TORRE D' ALTA MAR
Passeig de Joan de Borbó Comte de Barcelona 88, Barcelona 34 932 210 007
http://www.torredealtamar.com
CUISINE: Catalan, Seafood
DRINKS: Full Bar
SERVING: Lunch & Dinner
PRICE RANGE: $$$$
NEIGHBORHOOD: Montjüic
Beautiful restaurant located at the top of a tower which offers incredible views. Great seafood (prawns and sea bass) also beef medallions. Matching wine list. Staff speak Spanish only. Reservations recommended.

XEMEI

Passeig de l'Exposició, 85, Barcelona, 34 935 535 140
www.xemei.es
CUISINE: Italian – Venetian
DRINKS: Full Bar
SERVING: Lunch & Dinner
PRICE RANGE: $$$
NEIGHBORHOOD: El Poble-sec
Intimate eatery offering delicious Italian fare, with an emphasis on the cuisine of Venice. Located just beneath Montjuic and a short distance from the Lliure and Mercat de les Flores theatres. Ask the waiter for olive oil – they will bring you a bottle of the oil they make themselves (you'll end up buying a bottle or two to take home). I never come here without getting the fresh anchovies in vinegar. Favorites: Octopus with Eggplant and Black ink squid spaghetti. Great Tiramisu. Reservations recommended.

XIRINGUITO ESCRIBÀ

Avenida Litoral 62, Barcelona, 34 932 210 729
xiringuitoescriba.com.
CUISINE: Paella/Seafood/Mediterranean
DRINKS: Full bar
SERVING: Lunch/Dinner
PRICE RANGE: $$$
NEIGHBORHOOD: La Vila Olímpica
Located near the beach, this very popular eatery specializing in Paella and seafood. Large portions. Reservations a must or put your name at the door and go for cocktails.

XIXBAR

Carrer de Rocafort, 19, Barcelona, 34 934 234 314
http://www.xixbar.com
CUISINE: Gin Bar
DRINKS: Full Bar
SERVING: Late Night; closed Sunday
PRICE RANGE: $$
NEIGHBORHOOD: L'Eixample
Of all the gin bars in all the world, this place may
have the best selection. About 100 different gins and
48 tonics. If you're not a gin and tonic fan, this place
will change your mind. Beautiful antique marble bar
counter.

INDEX

Q

R

S

T

W

X

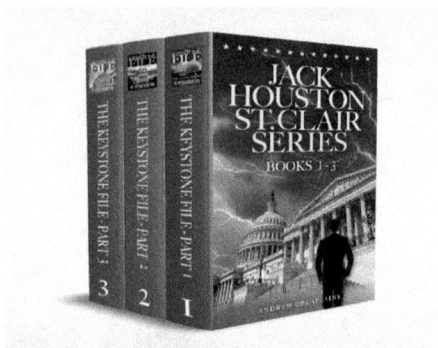

WANT 3 *FREE* THRILLERS?

Why, of course you do!
If you like these writers--
Vince Flynn, Brad Thor, Tom Clancy, James Patterson,
David Baldacci, John Grisham, Brad Meltzer, Daniel
Silva, Don DeLillo
If you like these TV series --
House of Cards, Scandal, West Wing, The Good Wife,
Madam Secretary, Designated Survivor

You'll love the **unputdownable** series about
Jack Houston St. Clair, with political intrigue, romance,
and loads of action and suspense.

Besides writing travel books, I've written political thrillers
for many years that have delighted hundreds of thousands
of readers. I want to introduce you to my work!
Send me an email and I'll send you a link where you can
download the first 3 books in my bestselling series,
absolutely FREE.
Mention **this book** when you email me.
andrewdelaplaine@mac.com

www.ingramcontent.com/pod-product-compliance
Lightning Source LLC
LaVergne TN
LVHW051151080426
835508LV00021B/2579

2020
BARCELONA
Restaurants

The Food Enthusiast's
Long Weekend Guide

Andrew Delaplaine

GET 3 FREE NOVELS
Like political thrillers?
See next page to download 3 FREE page-turning
novels—no strings attached.

Andrew Delaplaine is the Food Enthusiast.
When he's not playing tennis,
he dines anonymously
at the Publisher's (considerable) expense.

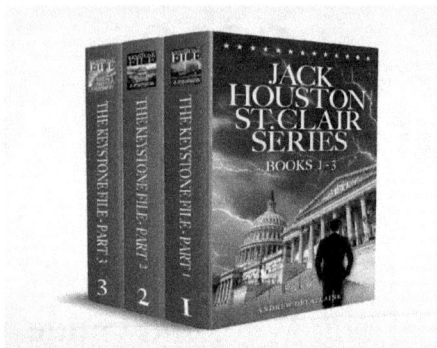

WANT 3 FREE THRILLERS?

Why, of course you do!
If you like these writers--
Vince Flynn, Brad Thor, Tom Clancy, James Patterson,
David Baldacci, John Grisham, Brad Meltzer, Daniel
Silva, Don DeLillo
If you like these TV series --
House of Cards, Scandal, West Wing, The Good Wife,
Madam Secretary, Designated Survivor

You'll love the **unputdownable** series about
Jack Houston St. Clair, with political intrigue, romance,
and loads of action and suspense.

Besides writing travel books, I've written political thrillers
for many years that have delighted hundreds of thousands
of readers. I want to introduce you to my work!
Send me an email and I'll send you a link where you can
download the first 3 books in my bestselling series,
absolutely FREE.
Mention **this book** when you email me.
andrewdelaplaine@mac.com